A Kid's Guide to
Origami™

Making
ORIGAMI CARDS
Step by Step

Michael G. LaFosse

The Rosen Publishing Group's
PowerKids Press™
New York

To my mother, Betty LaFosse

Published in 2004 by The Rosen Publishing Group, Inc.
29 East 21st Street, New York, NY 10010

First Edition

Editor: Jannell Khu
Book Design: Emily Muschinske
Layout Design: Michael J. Caroleo

Photo Credits: All photos by Adriana Skura.

LaFosse, Michael G.
Making origami cards step by step / Michael G. LaFosse.— 1st ed.
    v. cm. — (A kid's guide to origami)
Includes bibliographical references and index.
Contents: What is origami? — Pocket card — Origami heart — Origami duck — Origami flower — Origami plant — Jack-o'-Lantern card — Origami pinwheel — Origami pineapple.
ISBN 0-8239-6701-8 (library binding)
1. Greeting cards—Juvenile literature. 2. Origami—Juvenile literature. [1. Origami. 2. Greeting cards. 3. Paper work. 4. Handicraft.] I. Title. II. Series.
TT872 .L34 2004
736'.982—dc21

                                            2002153458

Manufactured in the United States of America

Contents

What Is Origami?

Origami is the art of paper folding to make shapes. In Japanese, *ori* means "fold," and *kami* means "paper." Chinese, Korean, and Japanese people have enjoyed origami for hundreds of years. Today people around the globe enjoy this art.

In Japan, it is **customary** to attach or paste an origami shape to a blank card. These origami cards are especially beautiful when placed on a simply wrapped gift. It is in the spirit of this origami gift-giving tradition that we present this book. Your family and friends will enjoy receiving origami cards that you have made especially for them!

Learning to follow the origami instructions in this book will be easier if you study the origami key at the back of this book on page 22. Notice the different folds, such as the mountain fold and the valley fold. Most of the folds in this book will be valley folds. Be sure to know the different kinds of arrows used to explain the folding directions. You can use many kinds of paper to make origami. Experiment with wrapping and copier papers. Some papers have a different color on each side. These papers are ideal for projects which show both sides of the paper when completed, such as the pocket card on page 7. If you are using colored origami paper, make sure the white side faces up before you start. You can use one shape for different greeting cards. For instance, you will learn how to make an origami heart on page 9. You can fold four of these hearts with green paper, then arrange them to make a **shamrock** for a St. Patrick's Day greeting card!

Pocket Card

A greeting card can be as simple as a folded sheet of paper. Most cards are folded so that a **personal** message can be written on the inside. Before there were machine-made papers and modern printing presses, greeting cards were handmade. Today most greeting cards are made by machine. This is why a handmade card is so special. You can make it even more special by decorating the card. This card is made with pockets. You can put movie tickets, a secret note, stickers, or even a stick of chewing gum inside the pockets. You can decorate the outside pocket by pasting on it the many origami shapes that you will learn how to make in this book.

1

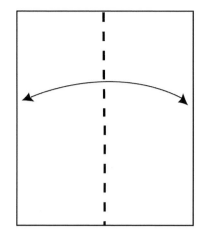

Take paper that measures 8 ½ inches (21.6 cm) by 11 inches (27.9 cm). Valley fold the paper in half lengthwise. Unfold. You have made a center crease line.

2

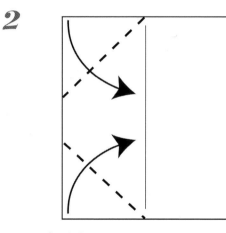

Valley fold the top and bottom corners on the left side to the crease line.

3

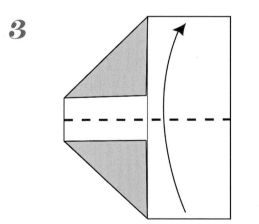

Valley fold the paper in half along dotted lines.

4

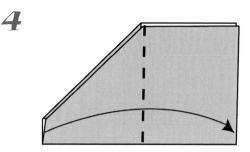

Valley fold the paper in half from left to right.

5

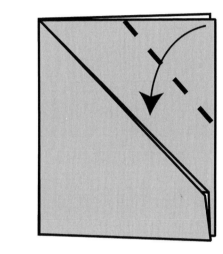

Valley fold down the top corner to make the point touch the folded edges of the front layers.

6

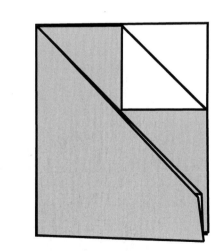

The finished card is now ready to decorate!

Origami Heart

   The heart shape stands for love in many countries. You can send cards decorated with hearts for many occasions, such as birthdays, Mother's Day, Father's Day, and, of course, St. Valentine's Day. If you love somebody, be sure to tell him or her often and in different ways. For instance, you can send loved ones cards with this heart design. Make several of these hearts and place them inside the pocket card you made in the previous chapter. Or paste an origami heart on a blank card and write "I love you" on top of the heart.

1

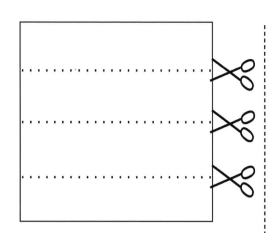

Use 6-inch- (15.2-cm-) square paper. Fold the paper into four equal parts and unfold. Cut the paper along the creases. You just made four equal-sized rectangles. These four rectangles will be used to make four hearts.

2

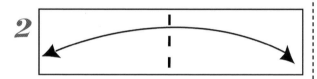

Valley fold one of the rectangles in half. Unfold.

3

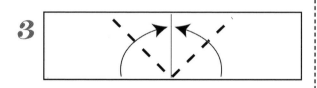

Valley fold the bottom left and the bottom right edges to make them meet at the center crease.

4

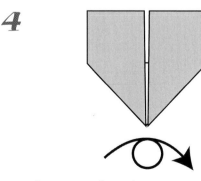

Turn the paper facedown.

5

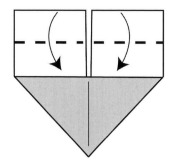

Valley fold down the top edges to match them to the edge of paper across the middle.

6

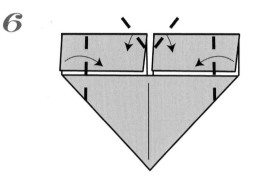

Fold down the two corners at the top center of the split. Valley fold the left and right edges, about a third of the distance to the center.

7

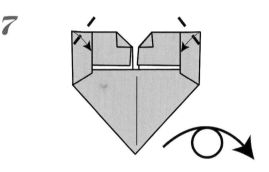

Valley fold down the corners at the top outside of the heart. Turn the paper over.

8

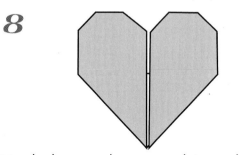

Use the heart to decorate a plain card or the pocket card you made in the last chapter.

Origami Duck

Mother ducks and their ducklings are a common sight in the spring in many places around the world. Cards decorated with origami ducks make nice Mother's Day cards or Easter cards. Ducks are very friendly to one another. Two ducks can stand for friendship. A card pasted with two ducks can be sent to friends to show how much you **appreciate** their friendship. This origami duck is easy to make. By experimenting with different ways of folding the angle of the duck's neck and head, you can make each duck look different.

1

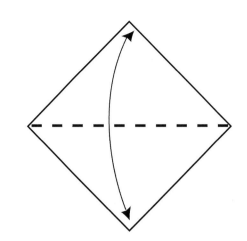

Use 6-inch- (15.2-cm-) square paper. Fold the first piece in half, corner to corner, and unfold to make a center crease.

2

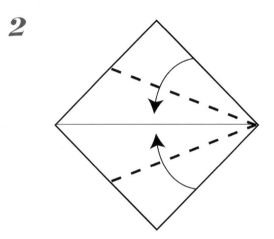

Valley fold the two edges toward the center crease line to make a kite shape.

3

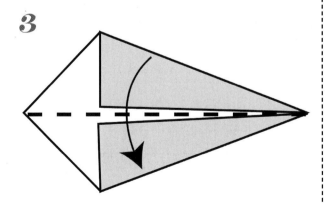

Valley fold in half, so that the folds are inside.

4

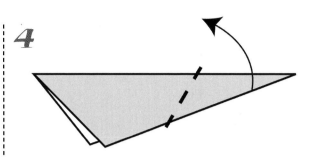

Valley fold up the narrow point to make the neck.

5

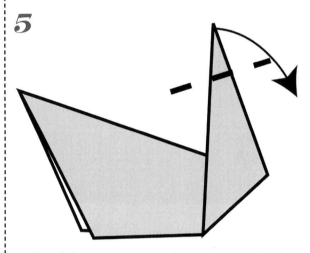

Valley fold down the end point to make the head.

6

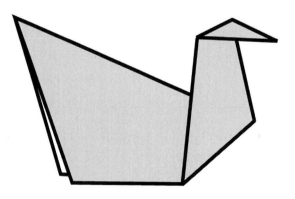

This is the finished duck. Be sure to apply glue to the body, the neck, and the head when you paste it to a card.

Origami Flower

    Flower cards are perfect for any occasion. Flowers grow in many different colors. Choose the color of your origami flower based on the season. Make red, white, and green origami flowers to decorate cards you will give during the winter. Orange and gold flowers are ideal for autumn. In the spring, make your origami flowers with soft, **pastel**-colored papers. Red and purple flowers can be used in the summer. You can make these origami flowers quickly and in any size. You can also try different folds on the petals.

1

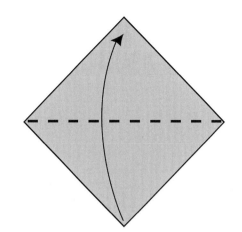

Use two 6-inch- (15.2-cm-) square papers. One of the papers should be green. The other can be any color of your choice. Take the paper that is not green and valley fold it in half, bottom corner to top corner.

2

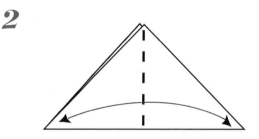

Valley fold the paper in half again, corner to corner. Unfold to make a center crease.

3

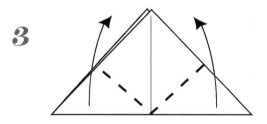

Valley fold up the two side corners toward the top corner. Corners should not be folded to meet at the center crease line, otherwise you will make a diamond shape. Look at step 4 to see how the shape should appear.

4

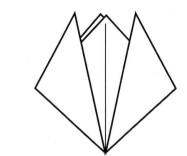

This is the basic flower shape. Next take the green colored paper and repeat steps 1 through 3. This is the stem of the flower.

5

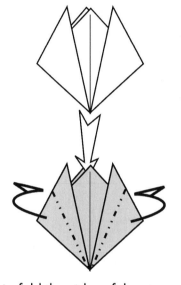

Mountain fold the sides of the stem around to the back. This will make the stem narrower than the flower. Push the flower into the top of the stem, between the two layers of the center corner.

6

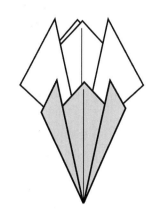

This is the finished flower. Try to shape the petals of the flower differently and see what other kinds of flowers you can create!

Origami Plant

Plants are **beneficial** to people. Plants produce oxygen. Oxygen is gas that has no color, taste, or odor and that is necessary for people and animals to breathe. This is why plants **symbolize** growth, **nourishment**, and **vitality**. This origami plant is useful to add to other origami shapes. For instance, this shape is used to complete the origami pineapple on page 21. Multiple origami plant shapes can be combined to make a Christmas tree or a sunburst pattern. Use your imagination, and see what else you can make with this origami plant shape.

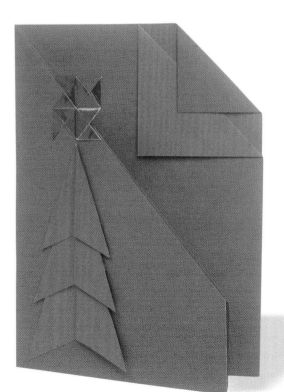

1

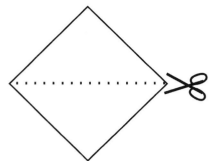

Use 6-inch- (15.2-cm-) square paper. Valley fold in half, corner to corner. Unfold. Cut along the crease lines as shown to make two triangles.

2

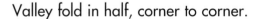

Valley fold in half, corner to corner.

3

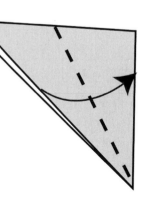

Position the triangle so that the folded edge is facing right. Hold the top layer, and valley fold to meet the folded edge.

4

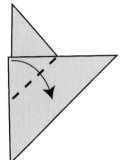

Turn the paper facedown.

5

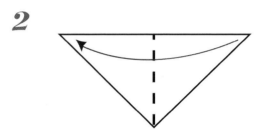

The paper will have one large triangle and a smaller one. Valley fold the left corner of the large triangle over to lock the layers together.

6

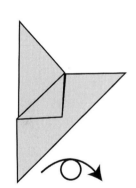

Turn the paper over.

7

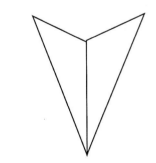

This is the finished shape. Use it to make a leaf, a plant, and tree shapes. You can also use it to make a star and a cross.

Jack-o'-lantern Card

Pumpkin origami cards are great to send to friends from Halloween through Thanksgiving. The pumpkin jack-o'-lantern is one of the most popular symbols of Halloween. Choose a bright orange paper for your origami jack-o'-lantern. Just as there are many jack-o'-lantern faces, there are many different **expressions** that you can give your origami jack-o'-lantern. Use your origami jack-o'-lanterns as decorations for Halloween or as invitations to a Halloween party. Have an origami folding contest at your party to see who can fold an origami jack-o'-lantern first!

1

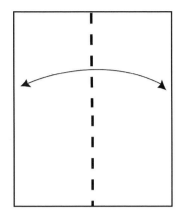

Use paper that is 8 ½ inches (21.6 cm) by 11 inches (27.9 cm). Valley fold lengthwise. Unfold it to create a center crease.

2

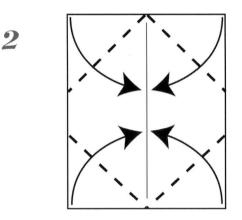

Carefully valley fold all four corners to the center crease. Look at the next step to see how your shape should appear.

3

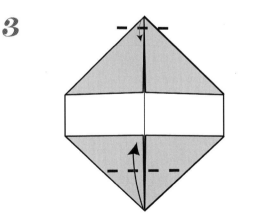

Valley fold the bottom corner so that it meets the base of the triangle at the center crease. Fold down the top corner a little bit to make it flat.

4

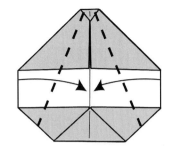

Valley fold the sides to meet in the middle. It should look like the shape below.

5

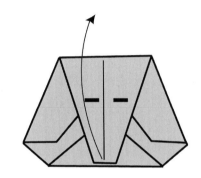

Valley fold in half, top to bottom.

6

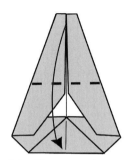

Valley fold up the part of the top flap of paper to make the stem.

7

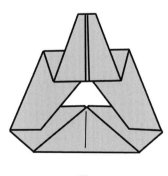

Turn it over. Look at the photograph on the opposite page to see how it should look. Draw a face on your pumpkin.

Origami Pinwheel

Many of us have played with pinwheels. We are familiar with their shapes and the way they spin. This simple origami toy is a great action toy. Pinwheels give us an excuse to go outside and enjoy a breezy day! Pinwheels are **marvels** of form and function. A well-built pinwheel can spin so fast that it becomes blurry and almost invisible! Brightly colored pinwheels made of shiny metal or plastic shine like sparklers on the Fourth of July. An origami pinwheel is a fun card decoration for celebrations such as New Year's Eve, birthdays, and **Independence** Day. Choose colorful paper to make origami pinwheels. Experiment with different ways to arrange your pinwheels.

1

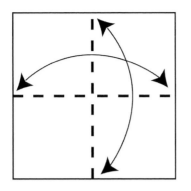

Use 6-inch- (15.2-cm-) square paper. Valley fold in half lengthwise. Unfold. Valley fold in half again from top to bottom. Unfold. You will have four squares.

2

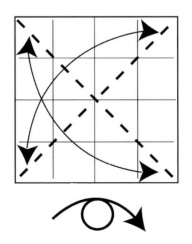

One at a time, valley fold and unfold each of the four edges to the center creases.

3

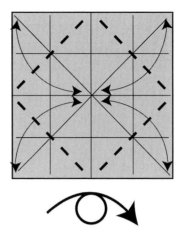

Valley fold in half, corner to corner, both ways. Unfold and turn the paper over.

4

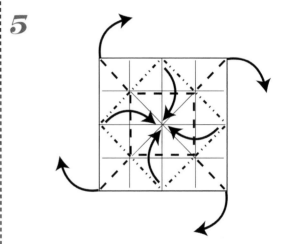

Valley fold each of the four corners to meet at the center. Unfold and turn the paper over.

5

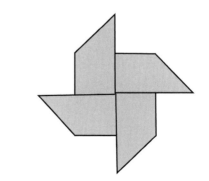

Using the creases that you made, move the middle of the edges of the square to the center while valley folding the corners in half. Make the pinwheel shape by mountain folding each corner down in a clockwise direction. Good work.

6

Your finished pinwheel should look as shown.

Origami Pineapple

Pineapples were brought to Europe from the Caribbean by Christopher Columbus. Pineapples were a rare treat in Europe. Only wealthy people could afford to buy pineapples. The display of a pineapple on the dinner table showed guests that they were invited to a special meal and that they were honored. This was how the pineapple came to stand for **hospitality**. Give pineapple cards to welcome a new neighbor or a new classmate. Origami pineapples also make nice baby shower cards to welcome the arrival of a new baby!

WELCOME

1

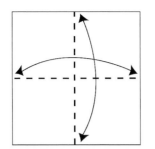

Use 6-inch- (15.2-cm-) square paper. Valley fold in half, lengthwise. Unfold. Fold in half top to bottom. Unfold.

2

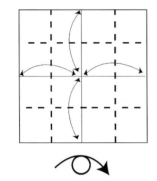

One at a time, valley fold and unfold each of the four edges to the center creases. Turn the paper facedown.

3

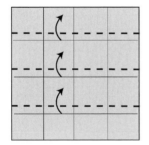

One at a time, fold each of the three horizontal creases so that they overlap a little of the paper above them.

4

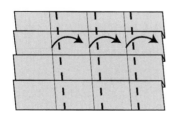

One at a time, grab each of the three vertical creases and valley fold them to the right, overlapping the paper.

5

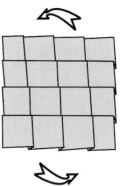

Rotate the paper to the diagonal position shown in step 6.

6

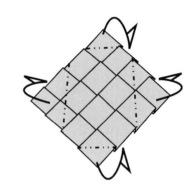

Mountain fold the four corners around to the back to make the pineapple shape.

7

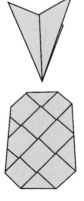

Paste the origami plant that you made on page 15 to the back of the pineapple.

Origami Key

1. MOUNTAIN FOLD

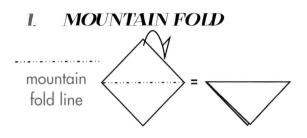

mountain
fold line

Notice the mountain fold line. To make a mountain fold, fold the paper back away from you, so that it meets at the other side.

2. VALLEY FOLD

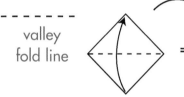

valley
fold line

Notice the valley fold line. To make a valley fold, fold the paper towards you.

3. MOVE, PULL, PUSH, SLIP

4. DIRECTION ARROW

5. FOLD and UNFOLD

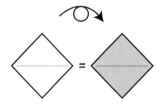

6. TURN OVER

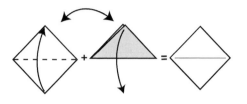

7. ROTATE

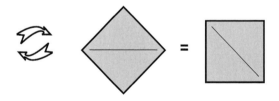

8. CUT

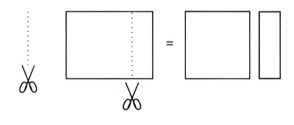

9. REPEAT

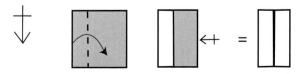

Glossary

appreciate (uh-PREE-shee-ayt) To be thankful for something or someone.

beneficial (beh-nuh-FIH-shul) Helpful; producing good.

customary (KUS-tuh-mer-ee) Commonly practiced.

expressions (ik-SPREH-shunz) Outward looks shown on the face.

hospitality (hos-pih-TA-luh-tee) The friendly treatment of guests.

independence (in-dih-PEN-dents) Freedom from the control or support of other people.

marvels (MAR-vulz) Wonderful or great things.

nourishment (NUR-ish-ment) Something needed for life and growth.

pastel (pa-STEL) A pale, soft shade of color.

personal (PERS-nl) Belonging to a person. Sometimes used to represent the private matters of a person.

shamrock (SHAM-rok) A clover leaf with three leaflets.

symbolize (SIM-buh-lyz) To stand for something else.

vitality (vy-TA-luh-tee) Lively life.

Index

Web Sites

Due to the changing nature of Internet links, PowerKids Press has developed an online list of Web sites related to the subject of this book. This site is updated regularly. Please use this link to access the list: www.powerkidslinks.com/kgo/greecard/